Machu Picchu

BY ELIZABETH RAUM

amicus
high interest

Amicus High Interest is an imprint of Amicus
P.O. Box 1329, Mankato, MN 56002
www.amicuspublishing.us

Library of Congress Cataloging-in-Publication Data
Raum, Elizabeth.
 Machu Picchu / Elizabeth Raum.
    pages cm. — (Ancient wonders)
 Summary: "Describes the mystery of Machu Picchu,
including how and why it was built, the emperor who lived
there, why it was abandoned, and what the ruin is like today"
—Provided by publisher.
 Includes bibliographical references and index.
 ISBN 978-1-60753-468-6 (library binding) —
 ISBN 978-1-60753-683-3 (ebook)
 1. Machu Picchu Site (Peru)—Juvenile literature. I. Title.
 F3429.1.M3R38 2015
 985'.37–dc23
                                2013028300

Editors   Kristina Ericksen and Rebecca Glaser
Series Designer   Kathleen Petelinsek
Book Designer   Heather Dreisbach
Photo Researcher   Kurtis Kinneman

Photo Credits
Herbert Eisengruber/Shutterstock, Cover; MIVA Stock/
SuperStock , 5; Keith Levit/Design Pics/SuperStock, 6; Michael
Langford/Getty Images, 8; National Geographic Image
Collection/Alamy, 10; VICTOR ENGLEBERT/SCIENCE PHOTO
LIBRARY, 13; Anton Ivanov/Shutterstock, 14; Anton Ivanov/
Shutterstock, 17; Robert Harding Picture Library/SuperStock,
19; James Edwin McConnell/Getty Images, 20; THOMAS
BLACKSHEAR/National Geographic Creative, 23; Hiram
Bingham/National Geographic Society/Corbis, 25; Glow
Images/SuperStock, 26; J Duggan/Shutterstock, 29

Printed in the United States of America at Corporate Graphics
in North Mankato, Minnesota.

10 9 8 7 6 5 4 3 2 1

Table of Contents

Ghost Town

Machu Picchu is called the "Lost City of the Incas." It's not lost anymore. But it is a ghost town. Nobody has lived there for over 500 years. All that remains are empty ruins. **Archaeologists** have studied the ruins. They know the Incas built Machu Picchu. But why? What did they do there?

 Are there really ghosts at Machu Picchu?

Machu Picchu is hidden in the mountains.

 No. A "ghost town" is a city that is abandoned.

Machu Picchu sits on a mountain in South America. It is in the country of Peru. Steep cliffs on three sides drop to the Urubamba River. Clouds swirl around the homes, fountains, and **temples**. Rain forests surround them. There is only one steep path up to Machu Picchu.

It is hard to reach these ancient ruins.

A King's Resort

The Incas lived in the Andes Mountains. They were a farming tribe. In about 1430, another tribe attacked. Pachacuti was a warrior. He led the Incas into battle. He drove out the enemies. The Incas were grateful. They made him **emperor**. Pachacuti expanded the **empire**.

This statue shows Pachacuti. He was an emperor of the Incas.

The Inca Empire got bigger during Pachacuti's rule. Stone paths and bridges connected cities.

 Q How big was the Inca Empire?

Pachacuti tried to get other tribes to join his. If they said no, he went to war. His empire grew. Over time, it included 12 million people. That's more people than live today in New York City and Los Angeles combined. Stone roads, rope bridges, and mountain paths connected the vast empire. Runners delivered messages.

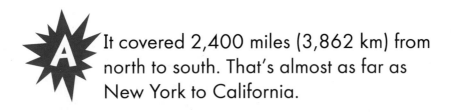
It covered 2,400 miles (3,862 km) from north to south. That's almost as far as New York to California.

Pachacuti lived in Cusco, the capital. In winter it was cold. Frost formed on trees. Archaeologists think Machu Picchu was Pachacuti's winter home. The mountain was warmer than Cusco. Pachacuti, his family, and servants stayed there for winter.

 What is the weather like at Machu Picchu?

Cusco has cold winters.

Machu Picchu is 50-85°F (10-29°C) all year. The nights are cool. The days are warm.

Machu Picchu is a week's walk from Cusco. To get there, people climbed the mountains. A beautiful view and lovely gardens awaited them. Pachacuti's friends and family had their own houses. They sat above the fountains and gardens. Pachacuti's house was set apart. It was more private.

Houses in Machu Picchu were made of stone.

15

Building Machu Picchu

No one knows how the Incas built Machu Picchu. They did not use iron tools. They did not use carts with wheels because it was so steep. But they were smart. They began building by turning the hillside into layered gardens, or **terraces**. It kept the land from washing away during heavy rains. Farmers grew corn and potatoes.

 When was Machu Picchu built?

The Incas made terraces on the steep land.

 It was built between 1450 and 1540.
It took about 90 years!

Next, they began building the houses. The Incas used llamas to carry supplies. But the huge stones were too heavy. Workers dragged them or rolled them on logs. They used smaller rocks to shape bigger ones. They chipped each one until it fit just right. Then they put the stones in place.

The Incas were masters at fitting stones together to make strong walls.

The Spanish invaded Peru
and took over Inca lands.

The Inca Empire lasted about 100 years. In 1532, Spanish explorers arrived. They destroyed Inca cities, killed leaders, and stole gold. Spanish diseases killed many Incas. But no one told the Spanish about Machu Picchu. They never found it. Machu Picchu fell into ruin.

The Lost City

In 1911, Hiram Bingham went to Peru. He was an American explorer. He talked with local people. They told him about the old ruins. A farmer told him to climb Machu Picchu, the "old peak." Bingham crossed the river on a shaky bridge. He climbed a steep path.

Hiram Bingham explored Machu Picchu in 1911.

At the top, he saw stone walls. Trees and bushes covered them. He pulled branches aside. He looked closer. He saw beautiful stone buildings. "Surprise followed surprise," he wrote.

In 1912 and 1915, Bingham returned. He wanted to learn more. There were no written signs to help him. The Incas did not have a written language.

 What language did the Incas speak?

Hiram Bingham took this picture
of Machu Picchu soon after he
discovered it.

 The Incas spoke Quechua. Some people in
Peru still speak it.

The ruins of the Temple of the Sun are still studied today.

 **Q** Are there still Inca people?

Machu Picchu Now

Archaeologists study the ruins today. They look for clues to understand Machu Picchu. For example, there are many temples. This shows that **religion** was important to the Incas. They called themselves "children of the sun." They worshipped the sun and mountains.

 Yes. The empire ended, but Inca people still live in Peru. They celebrate Inca history and festivals.

In 2011, more than one million people visited Machu Picchu. It is the biggest tourist site in Peru. Tourists climb the stone paths. They explore the gardens. They wander through empty houses. There are no ghosts at Machu Picchu. But there are still mysteries to solve.

 How do people get there today?

Many people today visit Peru and walk the same trails the Incas did.

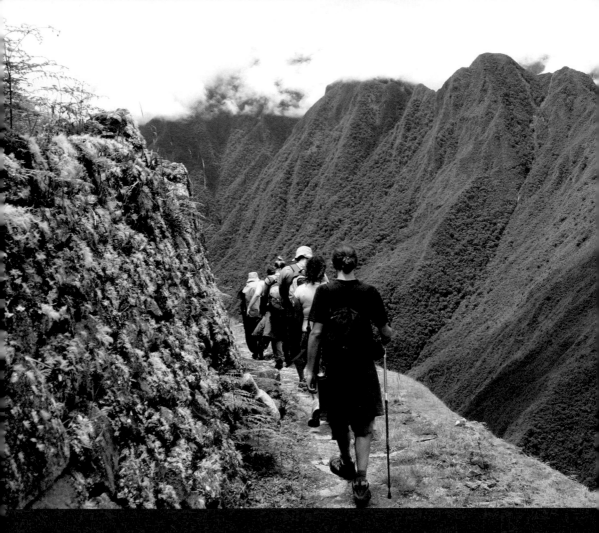

 Most people take a train from Cusco. It's a short walk from the station to the ruins.

Glossary

archaeologist A scientist who studies the remains of ancient people.

emperor A ruler or king.

empire A group of nations ruled by an emperor.

religion A belief in a god or gods with higher powers.

temple A place of worship.

terrace A flat platform on the side of a steep hill, used for farming.

Read More

Newman, Sandra. *The Inca Empire.* New York: Children's Press, 2010.

Riggs, Kate. *Machu Picchu.* Mankato, Minn.: Creative Education, 2009.

Sohn, Emily. *Investigating Machu Picchu: an Isabel Soto Archaeology Adventure.* Mankato, Minn.: Capstone Press, 2010.

Websites

Destination: Machu Picchu
http://www.peru-machu-picchu.com/

Machu Picchu — Panorama Photo
*http://www.panoramas.dk/fullscreen6/
f2-machu-picchu.html*

**Peru Facts and Pictures—
National Geographic Kids**
http://kids.nationalgeographic.com/kids/places/find/peru/

Index

About the Author

Elizabeth Raum has worked as a teacher, librarian, and writer. She has written dozens of books for young readers. She likes doing research and learning about new topics. After writing about ancient wonders, she wants to travel the world to visit them! To learn more, visit her website at www.elizabethraum.net.